**Genre** Histori

 Essential Quest
How can weather affect us?

The Big Storm

by Kate Sinclair • illustrated by Trystan Mitchell

CHAPTER 1

Trouble on the Horizon

"It's time to go," I called to Henry. My brother was always making us late in the mornings, and I didn't want to argue with him again.

"I'm almost ready, Loretta," Henry answered. "I'm just getting my marbles—I'm playing Billy at lunch."

As we left home, I noticed it seemed dark outside. There were big, black clouds in the distance. It looked like it was going to rain cats and dogs.

The walk to school usually took us thirty minutes, but today I wanted to get there quicker. I didn't like the look of those clouds, and I didn't want to arrive at school dripping wet. Henry was just ambling along, kicking at stones in the road.

"Let's hurry," I said to my brother. "We need to get to school before the rain starts."

Suddenly, the sky seemed to get even darker. Then I saw it. Far off in the distance, a big twister had formed. The twister was moving toward us!

"Oh no, Henry, look!" I said, pointing to the twister. "It's coming our way!" I was terrified.

Henry grabbed my hand. "Don't worry," he said. "We're still close to home. We can hurry back and tell Ma and Pa."

Big fat raindrops began to fall on us as we ran home. Then lightning jumped out the side of the twister. My heart was racing. The conditions were getting worse.

"Don't be scared. We're nearly there," Henry said, squeezing my hand.

We both called loudly to Ma and Pa as we ran up the pathway to our house.

"There's a storm coming!" Henry said as we burst through the front door.

"It's a twister!" I added, breathlessly.

Ma and Pa were astonished. They hadn't even noticed.

"Quickly, children," Ma cried. "We need to go down into the cellar—now!"

STOP AND CHECK

Why did Loretta and her family go to the cellar?

CHAPTER 2

The Storm Arrives

We rushed down the steps to the cellar, and Pa fastened the latch behind us. It was dark, and I was scared. What would happen if the twister ruined our house? I didn't want to be stranded in this cold, underground place.

Pa lit four candles. It wasn't dark anymore, but it was still cold, and I was still miserable.

"Come on, sis, cheer up," Henry said. "Everything will turn out okay; you'll see."

"But listen to the storm," I complained. The wind was blowing hard. It was whistling and screaming above us in our hiding place.

"Watch this!" said Henry, and then he put his hands in front of the candlelight.

Suddenly there was a dog on the wall! Then there was a goat, and after that, a rabbit.

"How did you do that?" I asked.

"It's easy," said Henry. "Come sit next to me, and I'll teach you how to do it."

Later, Henry and I were so busy laughing at the animal shadows we were making that we didn't notice the silence around us.

"Listen," said Pa. We all listened carefully.

"It's over," said Ma.

Pa crept upstairs to see how our house had stood up to the storm.

"It's all clear. You can come up," he called to us after a few minutes. I could hear relief in his voice.

STOP AND CHECK

How did Henry distract his sister?

CHAPTER 3

Making the Best of Things

"There's almost no damage to the house," Pa said. "I'll have to fix one or two of the shutters, but that's all. We've been very lucky."

"We should check on our neighbors," Ma said. "I hope they've been as lucky as us."

Ma, Pa, Henry, and I set off down the road, heading toward the center of town. As we got closer, we saw buildings and cars that had been badly damaged by the twister.

"Ma," I cried. "Look at that car. It's back-to-front. It looks like a toy that someone has picked up and thrown down somewhere else."

"That's what twisters do. The wind is so strong that it can pick up large things. Then it dumps them down again later," Ma said.

"This is terrible," Pa said as we looked around the town. There were roofless buildings, wrecked cars, and papers scattered about the streets. All of the other people who had come out to survey the damage looked as shocked and dazed as we felt.

Then I noticed the new girl from my class walking toward us with her ma. Her family had just moved to town. I saw that she was crying.

"What's your name?" I asked her.

"Bonnie," she said through her tears.

"What's wrong, Bonnie?" I asked.

"We've lost my brother," she said.

"I forbid him to go outside when I heard the weather forecast, but then he went out anyway," Bonnie's ma said.

"We'll help you look for him," I said. I felt so sorry for Bonnie. She was pale with worry.

"How old is your brother?" I asked Bonnie.

"He's ten," she said, "and he's old enough to know better!"

Just then, Henry yelled, "Look!"

We all turned to look in the direction in which Henry was pointing. There, huddled in a shop doorway, was a young boy.

"Is that him?" I asked, but Bonnie and her ma were already running across the street.

"It must be him," Henry said. "Let's go see if there is anything else we can do to help."

Now I felt sorry for Bonnie's little brother. He was relieved to see his family, but suddenly there were four strangers staring down at him as well. He was sobbing quietly, and we were all talking at once.

"Are you okay?"

"You poor thing!"

"Safe and sound at last!"

The boy looked up at us. "I couldn't get home," he said. "The twister came down the street so fast."

"You were lucky," his ma said. "This shop is unharmed, but our house is in ruins."

"Then you must come home with us," said my father.

"No, no," said Bonnie's ma. "We'll make do. We don't want to be a bother to anyone."

"Please don't argue," said Pa. "We have more than enough room. We are happy to have you and your family come stay with us for as long as you need."

I was happy about this idea, too. I knew that Bonnie and I would become great friends.

STOP AND CHECK

How did Loretta and her family help Bonnie?

Summarize

Use details from the story to summarize the important events in *The Big Storm*.

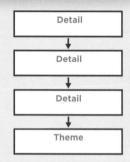

Text Evidence

1. How can you tell that this story is historical fiction? Identify one feature that tells you this. GENRE

2. What is the theme of this story? Look on pages 4 and 5 and pages 12–15 for clues. THEME

3. What does the phrase "stood up to" on page 8 mean? Use clues in the text to find out. IDIOMS

4. Write about the details the author used to communicate the theme, or message, of the story. WRITE ABOUT READING

Compare Texts

Read about how the weather affected an oak tree and some reeds.

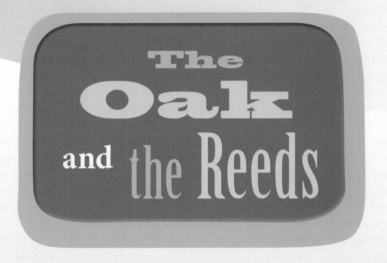

Once there was a large oak tree growing beside a stream. Some thin reeds also grew beside the stream. The oak stood proudly with its arms lifted toward the sky. The reeds bowed and swayed in the wind.

One day, the grand oak tree spoke to the reeds. "Why don't you grow roots deep into the soil? Then you will be able to stretch up toward the sky like me," the oak tree said.

"We may not be grand like you," the reeds replied, "but we are happy, and we are safe."

"Safe!" said the oak tree. "The smallest breeze makes you bow your heads. I stand proud and upright in the strongest winds. Who could uproot me or bow my head to the ground?"

"Do not worry about us," said the reeds. "We bow before the winds so we won't break. You stand firm and fight against the winds, so you are in more danger."

The next day, a big hurricane arrived. The reeds danced and bowed low in the winds.

The winds grew even more ferocious. Then suddenly, a strong gust tore the great oak tree out by its roots. It crashed down heavily beside the reeds.

"You see?" said the reeds to the fallen oak tree. "Sometimes you must stoop to conquer. The smallest can win out against the strongest of forces!"

Make Connections

What part did the weather play in *The Oak and the Reeds*? ESSENTIAL QUESTION

How can weather affect us? Use examples from *The Big Storm, The Oak and the Reeds*, and your own life to support your response. TEXT TO TEXT

Focus on Genre

Historical Fiction Historical fiction tells a story that is set in the past. The setting is realistic and drawn from history. Historical fiction sometimes contains real people from the past, but the main characters are usually made up.

Read and Find *The Big Storm* tells a story that happened in the past. The author learned the true stories of people who were affected by tornadoes in the first half of the 1900s and used facts from those real events to write this story.

Your Turn

Find out about a weather event that happened in the past in your town or state. Write a story set in the past using the facts you have learned. Have your characters do things that people in that time might have done.